Mighty Men of Valor

A Book of Encouragement and Prayer

Erica and Lewis Rutherford, Jr.

Edited by: Claude R. Royston

BK

ROYSTON
Publishing

BK Royston Publishing
P. O. Box 4321
Jeffersonville, IN 47131
502-802-5385
http://www.bkroystonpublishing.com
bkroystonpublishing@gmail.com

Cover Design: Brent Barnett
Cover Image © Crystalcraig | Dreamstime.com Used
with permission and license

ISBN-10: 1-946111-01-5
ISBN-13: 978-1-946111-01-2

Printed in the United States of America

Dedication

We dedicate this book to every man in this hour that needs encouragement, empowerment and strength as they go through life's issues and challenges. Our goal with this book is to bring just that. So this book is for you.

Acknowledgements

First, We acknowledge and give all honor to our Lord and Savior Jesus Christ for giving us all the words to write this book and for gifting us both with the gift to write His words.

To our family and friends that have encouraged and supported us in our marriage journey as we have sought to do God's will in everything that we have done. We will continue to do great things.

Introduction

The Purpose of this Encouragement Book is to strengthen and empower Men who are hurting, misunderstood, discouraged, and going through the twists and turns of life. May this book give you strength for your everyday life, nourish your soul, rekindle the fire in your spirit and renew your mind, so that you can stand in the whole armor of God against the enemy.

There is such a great need for Men to be encouraged in this hour. God placed a heavy burden on upon the heart my wife and me to write this small encouragement and prayer book. We want you to read this book as many times as you desire. Take time to read and meditate on the words within. It is our prayer that you will be encouraged and empowered today by God's word. Along with reading your bible, we encourage you to add this to your list of books of encouragement reading. We invite and encourage you to share this book with other men in your life or circle that could use it. We pray God's blessings upon you as you read it and that it would bless your soul.

AND REMEMBER: "YOU ARE A MIGHTY MAN OF VALOR." GOD BLESS YOU.

Erica and Lewis Rutherford, Jr.

Day 1

Men of Courage

Joshua 1:5 (KJV)
"No man shall be able to stand before you all the days of your life. As I was with Moses, so I will be with you; I will not fail you or forsake you."

There are times in our lives when we are in fear to some degree. For example, when it comes to standing for what is right when others choose to do the wrong thing or being the new leader on a job when you know others don't respect or listen to you. Even just being the man that God wants us to be in a world where the morals we grew up learning now have become a fading trend. But through all these times in our lives, God is with us no matter how tough our road is. He says, he will see us through it and we will come out victorious. The thing is that we must have the courage to trust, lean on God and allow God to get us through it. Being a man of courage doesn't mean that we have to be FEARLESS; because he knows we will fear and worry sometimes. Being a man of courage means: despite my worries and my fears, I put my trust in God to see me through it and bring me out victorious. He is God. He won't fail me nor leave me in the things I fear and worry about. God is with me.

1

Prayer of the Day

Lord, you are the head of my life, my King of kings and Lord of lords. Help me to be a man of courage and of strength. To trust you in everything that I fear and worry about and to continue to know that you are with me and that you won't fail me. Let your word be written on the tablet of my heart. To know that you haven't given me the spirit of fear but power, love, and a sound mind. As I am strengthened, help me to encourage and strengthen others. In Jesus name I pray, Amen.

Day 2

The Call of A Peacemaker

1 Samuel 24:4-7 (KJV)
(Take a moment to read these scriptures.)

Mighty Man of Valor, in this season you are called to be a peacemaker. In a world where we are surrounded by violence, the natural instinct of a man when threatened by violence is to fight/retaliate. Why? Because men are protectors. When they feel their safety is threatened, the first thing that usually comes to mind is to eliminate the threat. But God's challenge to you Man of Valor, is for you to be like David. David in 1st Samuel 24:2-7, had a chance to kill Saul his leader, but he spared him. Logically speaking, David had every reason to take advantage of the opportunity given to him. But he chose not to, but he did in fact cut off a portion of his leader's robe. In scripture, you find that David is indeed sorrowful even for doing that. Why? Because he had a good heart. He loved his leader. His leader during this time became his enemy. But God in this season is calling for you to be a peacemaker just like David tried to be. Matthew 5:9 says: "Blessed are the peacemakers. For they shall be called Sons of God." Yes, Man of Valor, you are called to be a peacemaker. You are needed to help stop the violence and not contribute to it. Your family needs you to come home at night. You are needed to be an

3

example in the earth. You are needed to bring peace and order in the earth. One of the ways you do that, is by your choice not to retaliate when violence seems to be pursuing you or is all around you. Know that vengeance is the Lord's. Romans 12:19 says to let God be your avenger and to see peace in every situation and circumstance where possible. Let God deal with your enemies.

Prayer of the Day

Lord God, help me each and every day to choose to be a peacemaker. Help me not to retaliate when wrong or evil is done to me or pursues me. Help me to have the same heart as David did to love my enemies. Help me to be a good example in front of my family, friends and all others around me. Help me to be more like you. In Jesus name I pray, Amen.

Day 3

He's Calling You

Matthew 22:14 (KJV)
"For many are called but few are chosen."

We as men have admired the people in the bible for how they go from being ordinary to extraordinary. We always looked at how God used them to lead his people out of circumstances and situations, how he chose individuals to rule as kings and judges and give them the power to overcome things that stood in their way. But we never looked at how they became what God called them to be. We as men must understand that each one of us must answer the call. Like Moses with the burning bush, he heard God calling him. Like David while tending to the sheep and in worship, God saw his heart and used the prophet Samuel to anoint him to be king. God uses us to do what he purposes our lives to be and to fulfill the reason why we are here on earth. The question is: 'Are we listening?' Have we really taken the time to ask him what is our calling and what we are here to do? God wants his sons to know that He has a plan and purpose for our lives. He wants us to answer the call. The question is: 'Will we as men be the one to answer?' For the harvest is great but the laborers are few, God wants us to be the one to answer. All it takes is a willing heart.

Prayer of the Day

Father, you have taken ordinary people and made them extraordinary. Now Lord, reveal the plan for my life and use me for your glory. Let me be the one who answers the call and lives a life pleasing in your sight. One who lives a life poured out in your service. In Jesus name I pray, Amen.

Day 4

My Plans For You

Jeremiah 29:11(NIV)
"For I know the plans I have for you, declares the
Lord. Plans to prosper you and not to harm you,
plans to give you hope and a future."

(NLT)
"For I know the plans I have for you, says the Lord.
They are plans for good and not for disaster, to give
you a future and a hope."

The word "Valor" means: boldness or determination
in facing great danger, especially in battle, heroic
courage and bravery. As a Man of Valor in this
corrupted world, much of what you see around you is
evil. There is hardly any good. When you do see
good, you try and take pleasure in it; enjoying that
moment. For you don't know how long it will last.
Tragedy happens every day. Life is running its
course daily as God graces you to wake up to see a
brand new day. In spite of what each day holds, you
should thank God every day and every moment for
his grace and for you to live and see it. Why?
Because tomorrow is not promised, not even the
next moment. What God wants you to know, is that
in the midst of all that is around you, His plan for you
is to prosper (thrive; flourish) you, not to harm. The
violent and destruction you see around you is not

7

what God originally intended. God's plans for you were plans of peace and well-being. God is a God of peace. And he desires that all have peace. But He also understands that because of the free will of man, that peace within the earth is greatly diminished. But in God, you Man of Valor can find and have peace and prosperity through God in a time when most people seem to struggle for it. For in Christ, you can find all things that you need. If you seek first the Kingdom of God and his righteousness, then all other things shall be added unto you. So seek God first and the things of God, then the things that you have the most concern for shall be taken care of.

Prayer of the Day

Heavenly Father, I pray daily that I will be the Man of Valor that you have called for me to be. Help me daily to be a Man of peace and to continuously seek you for the peace and prosperity that only you can give. I realize that what I see before me is not what you originally desired, but thank you Lord for your plans. I am thankful that I can put my full hope and trust in you. Help me to trust your way and will for my life. In Jesus name I pray, Amen.

Day 5

A Place Of Surrender

Proverbs 3:5-6 (KJV)
"Trust in the Lord with all thine heart; and lean not
unto thine own understanding. In all thy ways
acknowledge him and he shall direct thy path."

In our everyday life, we as men always fill our hearts
and minds with the situations and circumstances of
the things we go through. We are always trying to do
things our way and hoping that it will work. We try
being the person who has it all together and who
knows it all. We are being men who are full of pride,
when clearly we don't have it all together. We try and
we become frustrated when it doesn't go the way we
thought it would go or when everything we do or try
to do doesn't work. Have you ever thought that it's
God's way of trying to get our attention? We as men
always want to be great in what we do and be
successful in life. But we fail to understand that we
can't live this life without God. So we need to
understand: that we need God in our everyday life, in
every step we take and in every move we make. Not
only the big things in our lives but also in the small
details of our lives. That requires us to empty out
ourselves and allow God to fill our hearts and minds.
We must also trust him. We as men must empty out
all the bitterness, the frustrations, the heartaches,
the stress, and the depressions of life. And we must

let God fill us with his peace, strength, love and joy in our lives, for God cares for us.

Prayer of the Day

Heavenly father, I empty out myself of my past hurts, pains, my perceptions and points of view. My frustrations, everyday stress, past relationships and people who've hurt me. I totally surrender it to you. Lord, fill me with your peace, your strength, your joy and love in my life. And renew my heart, my mind and my spirit. In Jesus name I pray, Amen.

Day 6

Chosen for Now

1 Samuel 16:11-13 (KJV)
(Take a moment to read these scriptures)

The word 'called' means: to ask or invite to come. The word 'chosen' means: selected from several; preferred elect. Man of Valor, you have been chosen to fulfill a great purpose in the earth. You are not just called- Matthew 22:14. God knew you from your mother's wound- Jeremiah 1:5. You were chosen for such a time as this- Esther 4:14. In the beginning, you were created by God to have rule and dominion in the earth such as Adam did. Concerning the time in which we are living in right now, you are called and chosen to be an example in the earth. An example of what, you say? An example of how a Man should take care of his family and his responsibilities. He should be an example of how a man should try to become all that is positive and pure. He should also be an example of how a man can be successful in spite of how society has labeled men. You are chosen because you are gifted. You have purpose. You are one-of-a-kind. You are unique, and you have been equipped with God's favor. In 1st Samuel 16:11-13 when Samuel sought to follow God's instructions to anoint the next King, he was not looking for a man that was of a certain appearance or height. He was not focused on outward appearance. But he was looking at the heart of the Man. The one that would be chosen would have the right heart. And all of the sons of Jesse did not meet the qualifications of who Samuel was looking for. There was only one. And that one was David. David was glowing with health and had fine appearance along with handsome features. Most importantly, he had the right heart condition that God was looking for. Today Man of Valor, you must realize that you too must possess high qualifications, just as David did to be chosen. How can you know you have been chosen? Look around you and amongst the world. Examine the threat that men pose to those of higher authority. Look at the struggle that men at times endure just because they are Men. Then, you can begin to understand why you have been chosen for such a time as this. You Man of Valor, have been chosen because of who you are. Know who you are and walk in your identity as a Man of Valor today. Be the example that others can look to as an example. For such a time as this, you have been called and chosen.

Prayer of the Day:

Heavenly Father, Thank you for your encouragement today concerning me. I am honored to be called your child. I am honored and humbled that you have called and chosen me for such a time as this. Now Lord, help me daily to be an example. Help my heart condition daily to be right with you. Lord, take out anything that is not like you. I am reminded daily who I am because of you. Help me to remember that always. Thank you Lord. In Jesus name I pray, Amen.

_____
_____
_____
_____
_____
_____
_____
_____
_____
_____
_____
_____
_____
_____
_____
_____
_____
_____
_____
_____
_____
_____

Day 7

A Spiritual Check Up

Psalms 26:2 (KJV)
"Examine me, O LORD and prove me; try my reins
and my heart."

It's amazing how we as men want to make sure that we are in good health. We go to the gym to exercise, eat or at least try to eat healthy and take the right vitamins for our body in order to function. We even get a checkup from the doctor to see if our health is good or if we need improvement. But do we as men ever have a Spiritual Checkup? To check to see if our hearts, our thoughts, how we treat people, our attitude towards life and everything we do and say is pleasing to God? Even in our hearts, minds, our walk and relationship toward him, we should want to be pleasing in his sight. Well here's a good tip for us! As much as we as men do a natural diagnosis on ourselves, we also need to do a spiritual diagnosis on ourselves. Take time for ourselves and spend that quiet time with God to check ourselves. For it will: help us understand why we as men feel the way we feel. Why we do the things we do. Things that can be: detrimental, cause us not to be in tune with God and have a calloused heart toward him. We as men must walk more in the spirit and not the flesh. We must be the Men that God called and purposed us to be!

15

Prayer of the Day

Father, help me to examine myself and allow me to see things that I need to work on. Things in me that is not of you. Take out of me even the secret and hidden things in my life, Help me to continually be in-tune and close to you and live a life poured out and pleasing to you. In Jesus name I pray, Amen.

Day 8

Your Gift Opportunity

Proverbs 18:16a (KJV)
"A man's gift maketh room for him.."

In 1st Samuel 16:21-23, David was blessed with a special talent of being able to play the harp (lyre). His profession was a shepherd or tender of sheep, which he did in his father's vineyard. In your profession, you may not always have the opportunity to use your talent or gift, but there is always a place for you. At some point in our lives, we are presented with an opportunity to use our gift or talent. And we must seize that opportunity. David's gift made room for him in his relationship with Saul. He became his armor bearer. David was needed for the very important task of playing his harp every time an evil spirit tried to disturb Saul. The talent of David was used to drive out evil tormenting spirits. David was also especially blessed and anointed by God which added to his success in accomplishing the task. You, Man of Valor have been blessed by God to use your God given talents. And your gifts and talents shall make room for you as well. There is a place and opportunity just for you. Don't be like the man that buried his talents. In Matthew 25:14-38, one of the servants was given one talent. In verses 24-25, that

17

servant hid his talent in the ground. He did not do anything with it like the other servants did. Therefore, his reward in the end was that his talent was taken away and given to the one with ten talents (vs 26-28). Talents back then represented money. Today, talents represent exactly what they are: talents. So the question is Man of Valor: What will you do with yours?

Prayer of the Day:

Lord, thank you for blessing me with the talents and gifts that you have given me. Lord, you have given me precious gifts and talents made especially for me. Lord, forgive me for not seizing opportunities presented to me to use those talents and gifts. Give me more opportunities. Help me daily to follow your leading and to hear your voice. Help me to continuously be encouraged that my gift will make room for me. Also help me not to bury my talents and gifts, but to use them for your glory. In Jesus name I pray, Amen.

Day 9

How U Speak, Is How U Live

Proverbs 18:20-21 (KJV)
"A man's belly shall be satisfied with the fruit of his mouth; and with the increase of his lips shall he be filled. Death and life are in the power of the tongue: and they that love it shall eat the fruit thereof."

Do we as men ever understand: the power of our words, the strength of them and the weight they carry when we speak them into people's lives? Do we understand the effects that they have, not only in the natural realm, but also in the spiritual realm? We as men must understand that we were made in the image and likeness of God. When he created the heavens and the earth, he spoke us into existence. So now, we as men must understand that our words have power. We must understand that what we say has an effect, it's whether it's negative or positive. For example: if we get up in the morning and say our day is going to be a hard day, then we go to work and everything is goes wrong. It's because we spoke it into existence. This is why God wants us to speak life and study his word; the word of God, so that we know and understand who we are in him. Also, the words we speak has an effect in people's lives. We can build, change, and make a difference in their lives or we can tear them down. So, if we are speaking negative in our own lives then negative

19

things will happen.
If we speaking positive in our own lives, then good things will happen. God understood this because when he spoke, things happened. So that is why we as men must know and understand the power of our words.

Prayer of the Day

Father, help me to speak life in myself, my family and others. And help me continue to know and understand the power of my words, and how what I say can have an effect. In Jesus name I pray, Amen.

Day 10

Do not Self-Promote, Do Not Run Ahead, But Wait on God.

(Proverbs 27:2)." NETB
"Let another praise you, and not your own mouth; someone else, and not your own lips"

It is crucial in this season and in this hour, that you do not self-promote and that you do not run ahead of God. Don't become anxious for things that you desire and want. Don't become impatient and try to make them happen quicker. Don't try to help God bring to pass the very thing that he promised that he would do for you as though He can't do it himself. Understand that moving and running ahead of God, will only get you in trouble. It will only cause your blessings to become strained. The full manifestation of what God had planned has now become hindered because of your impatience and anxiety. Don't cause yourself to be delayed. Don't risk having to start the process over again because of your own impatience. In looking at the story of David, David's fame was a result of him fulfilling his mission in life. Now when David messed up; when he failed, he repented and asked God's forgiveness. And when he was successful, he acknowledged God. Never throughout David's story do you see or find David exalting himself over the Lord. Why? Because David knew better. He knew who was responsible for all his success. He knew who was to get all the glory, honor and the praise. So, the Word of God says in 1 Chronicles 14:17: "So David's fame spread through every land, and the LORD made all the nations fear him." So it clearly noted that 'The Lord' is who caused his fame to spread through the land, and made all the nations fear him. David just was a vessel that the Lord used. So Man of Valor, the Lord has a message for you today. Man of Valor, wait on God. Be still and know that He is God. Rid yourself of anxiety and worry. Rebuke the false hunger "that you have to have this or that right now." For the Lord is saying: "Yes, This Is Your Time, but, let me bring you into your time. Allow me to be your self-promoter. Stand still and know that your gifts, talents and abilities will make room for you in the marketplace and in the kingdom.' "Let another praise you, and not your own mouth; someone else, and not your own lips (Proverbs 27:2)." So Man of Valor, Don't Self Promote, Don't Run Ahead, Don't get anxious in well doing, but stand and wait on God. Seek Him and you will never go wrong. Psalms 37:23 says: "the steps of a good man are ordered by the LORD, and he delights in his way." - Selah

Prayer of the Day

Lord, forgive me for any times that I have promoted myself or ran ahead of you. Forgive me for not waiting on you. Lord, help me to trust you in the process of you promoting me to where you will have me to be. Lord, help me to seek you in everything that I prepare to set out to do for you. Lord, I want you to be in everything. I will let others praise me and not me myself. I will continuously give all honor to you. Help me in the times I get anxious in well doing to wait on you. In Jesus name I pray, Amen.

Day 11

Casting Our Crowns and Worship

Matthew 5:7, 9 (KJV)
"Blessed are the merciful: for they shall obtain mercy. Blessed are the peacemakers: for they shall be called the children of God."

It's always a challenge when we as men have power and don't use it properly. We often get prideful and arrogant. Trying to rule with an iron fist instead of a lending hand to people who really need help. We as men must rule with love and grace like Christ did. When the world says we have every right to condemn, Christ says show grace and mercy. Just like the woman in the bible that committed adultery, the Pharisees said stone her because of the law. But Christ said, show mercy and grace towards her. Having power doesn't mean that we become a dictator. It means that we are capable of: ruling, maintaining peace and becoming a great leader. Whether it's a business or just at home, we as men must learn how to rule like the elders in heaven. Having a crown but casting it at Christ's feet and worshipping him. We as men must submit and humble ourselves before God and learn to depend on his wisdom to lead well.

Prayer of the Day

Lord, your ways are higher than my ways and your thoughts are higher than my thoughts. Help me to be a leader that leads well. Give me the wisdom to be a great leader in my home, job and church. Allow me to glorify you in all that I do. In Jesus name I pray, Amen.

Day 12

When Others Fail You

2 Corinthians 5:18: (KJV)
"And all things *are* of God, who hath reconciled us to himself by Jesus Christ, and hath given to us the ministry of reconciliation."

There is a devotional called: "When Others Fail You" by O. S. Hillman out of the Marketplace Meditations 'Today God Is First Series" that stirs this message to you today Man of Valor. The devotion talks about encouraging those around you that may have seem to fail you when you needed them the most. *The original devotion is based upon the fact that an executive in the owner's company attempted a corporate takeover. But he was unsuccessful in doing so. Afterward, the owner still had to manage the same people who tried to take over his company.* Take time to read it when you get a chance. Today, we are going to look at how Jesus handled his disciples when they failed him as they journeyed with him. Jesus had many experiences with his disciples. Jesus already knew what he would have to endure with them. He also knew the true heart of the disciples. He knew they would flee when he was crucified, and he knew Peter would deny him 3 times. But in the end, Jesus still restored the disciples. Not by focusing on their failures and mistakes, but by building them up to continue on with the mission and purpose that was set before them. In John 20:21-22, Jesus spoke: "Again Jesus said, 'Peace be with you! As the Father has sent me, I am sending you." Jesus used grace and total acceptance as motivation for his followers to carry on the mission. Such was needed for them to be encouraged in their journey ahead. Such was the same with the man who had to continue to work with the employees of his company that failed him in the devotional. He had to rally his team together and help get them back on track with the vision and goal of the company. He had to build them up even after the failure. So the overall message of this devotional was: When Others Fail You, Restore the Peace and Send Them Forth. Wow! What a powerful message. This is what God is saying to you today. The most powerful thing that you can do after someone fails you is to restore them. 2 Corinthians 5:18 says: "And all things *are* of God, who hath reconciled us to himself by Jesus Christ, and hath given to us the ministry of reconciliation." That's what you are called to do Man of Valor. Will you make that choice today and also allow God to heal and restore you?

Prayer of the Day:

Lord, help me to take heed to your word by restoring my brothers and sisters when they fail me. I realize that life is not over and that it's not the end of the world. But also Lord, I still need to be healed. Lord, I ask that you would heal me in order that I may have the heart to restore my brother. Today, I just want to reconcile and not retaliate. Thank you Lord for your example. In Jesus name I pray, Amen

_____
_____
_____
_____
_____
_____
_____
_____
_____
_____
_____
_____
_____
_____
_____
_____
_____
_____
_____
_____
_____
_____
_____

Day 13

Man Moments with God

Hebrews 4:15-16 (KJV)
"For we have not a high priest which cannot be touched with the feeling of our infirmities; tempted like as we are, yet without sin. Let us therefore come boldly unto the throne of grace that we may obtain mercy and find grace to help in time of need."

Men, have you ever felt like there are things you go through that no one understands or things that made you feel misunderstood? Well we as men go through that and that's why it's so important that we draw closer to God; just have a heart to heart talk with him. God is our heavenly father and he longs to spend time with his children. Come to him just like a son that would come to his father. God loves and cares for his sons and wants us to spend time with him. Talk to him from what's in our hearts, on our minds and how we feel, we can talk to God about anything. God is not the type of God who we talk and pray to and he doesn't answer back. He talks to us just like we talk to him. The question is: Do we as men quiet ourselves and listen? Do we have a place where we spend that quiet time to hear God? Just as much as we praise and worship and study the bible, we also need to spend time in prayer. That is where we can talk to God and he talks to us. It doesn't have to be flashy or intellectual, but is like a son talking to

31

his father and a father talking to his son; heart to heart. Whatever is going on in our lives, God is always there. Even though he knows all and sees all, he still wants us to take the time to come and talk to him. God loves us with an everlasting love, and he longs to spend time with us. Just like we as parents love to spend time with our kids.

Prayer of the Day

Father, thank you for your love and care for me. Thank you for being the God that I can talk to no matter what's going on in my life. Thank you for being the father who longs to be with his children. Continue to draw me closer to you to spend more time. Not only in worship, praise and your word but also in prayer daily that I delight myself in you. For you are the center of my life. In Jesus name I pray, Amen.

Day 14

Does Your Devotion Exceed Your Service?

Proverbs 16:2 (KJV)
"All a person's ways seem pure to them, but motives are weighed by the Lord."

"Stay at my feet. Return back to me. Do you think you have all the answers? Do you need me anymore? Everything I the Lord your God is building up in this hour is being done with discreet instructions. The key to receiving the instructions is to sit at my feet and learn. Even my son Jesus, sought me continuously. He never stopped seeking me, even up to his dying day. Many are serving, but many have lost their devotion to me. In my name they go forth and try and just ask my blessing on what they are doing. But their devotion to seek me first is no longer. Many are running on what they think they know and not on my divine discreet instructions. Their heart to hear my voice has diminished. They want only my hand and not my heart. Therefore, my people have become distracted with service; they have neglected their devotion to me. Spending time with me has become distinct. Just sitting quietly, meditating without acknowledgment, repentance, worship and communication passes only for the motion of appearing spiritual. The act of seeking me through

33

the mentioned process involves patiently waiting to hear my heart and my voice. This represents pure devotion. Many want my hand and favor, but not the sharing of my heart and instructions. They proceed based on their own understanding. They acknowledge their own ways and direct their own paths. But they just try and add my name to it. Just add "Jesus on it" and you will have a finished product as though I was only a topping. I should comprise every ingredient, element and layer of your life. Then some criticize those that do seek true devotion or have true devotion with me by saying: "it doesn't take all that" or "why do you have to pray about it?"

Why criticize them? Because they want me involved in as much of if not all every detail of their life as possible. For each of those persons, I am every important in their lives. The element of devotion is real in their lives. So it is time for my people to cross examine themselves and their lives. You need to ask yourself: Man of Valor, are you spending time doing service; being busier with stuff than with spending quality (real) devotional time with me? Does your service exceed your devotion? Where am I on your priority list? Are you moving based on your own knowledge and understanding? Is every action or movement the result of discreet instructions and/or communication and devotion with me? -Selah

Prayer of the Day:

Lord, help me to daily balance my service with my devotion to you. Lord, forgive me for lacking in my devotion to you. I ask you to fix my balance so that I am not moving according to my own will and understanding, but on yours. Help me not to be so busy that I forget about you. Help me to keep you Lord first on my list at all time. In Jesus name I pray, Amen.

_____
_____
_____
_____
_____
_____
_____
_____
_____
_____
_____
_____
_____
_____
_____
_____
_____
_____
_____
_____
_____
_____
_____
_____

Day 15

An Oasis In The Desert

John 4:14 (KJV)
"But whosoever drinketh of the water that I shall give him shall never thirst; but the water that I shall give him shall be in him a well of water springing up into everlasting life."

There are times and seasons in our lives when we as men are in a dry spot. There's no progress or movement, and the things that we used to be passionate about fades. There are many things we try to do that doesn't satisfy us. They make us feel unfulfilled. We all go through that as men. Wondering, are the things in our lives in what we accomplished and done makes our lives fulfilling? Do we have a poured out life?
Jesus is saying in this scripture, that he is life and that you can't live a life without him. For it is Christ who makes our lives fulfilled and worth living. Just as much as he is the bread of life when we are hungry, he is also the water of life when we are thirsty. Jesus is life and in his presence there is fullness of joy, peace and love. There is freedom and a place where we can go away from all life's stresses and rest in him. It is in his presence where we as men are revived, rejuvenated, refresh and renewed. It is his presence that is an oasis in our dry times and seasons of our lives. All it takes is to worship to go

there. Letting the Holy Spirit dwell in us more and more each day, and there we will see our everlasting well that never runs dry.

Prayer of the Day

Lord, help me to spend more time in your presence each day and have more of your spirit in me that I will never thirst again. For you are the living water that never runs dry. When there are times that I'm in a dry spot in my life, I will worship and dwell in your presence. For everything I need is in your presence. Let your living water fill me and overflow. In Jesus name I pray, Amen.

Day 16

God Is Able to Keep You From Falling

Jude 1:24-25 (NIV)
"To him who is able to keep you from falling…….."

In a world where temptation is all around, where men struggle to stay pure and upright. Overcoming temptation is not always easy in a 'right now' society. But God says to you Man of Valor that you cannot overcome alone. You use your will, your intellect, your prestige, your own wisdom to help make everyday decisions. Your expectation is that the end result will be one of success. But while you may have some success, only one person is able to make sure that you are successful each and every time. That person is Jesus Christ. God's word contains your basic instructions of life. It even contains examples of individuals that dealt with similar issues and situations. Finally, it also contains instructions on how to overcome. But all credit in overcoming any temptation and the continuous battles of remaining in an overcoming state, belongs to God. Credit in the book of Judah gives honor and acknowledgment to Jesus; 'To him.' God has all the ability necessary to keep you from falling. Falling from what? Falling back to old habits and ways, and keeping you from retreating back to things that held you bound. What is impossible with you, is possible with God. For all

39

things are possible with God. The only one that holds all things in his hands is the one that is able to keep you from going backwards. His desire is that you would continue moving forward. Continue moving forward in life with Christ being your guide. Because of Christ's ability, he also empowers you with his ability and continuous guidance keeping you from falling. Will you Man of Valor, allow him to help keep you from falling? Will you give honor and acknowledgment to the one who is able to keep you from falling? To Christ, our only wise God who is able to keep you from falling. -Selah

Prayer of the Day

Lord, sometimes the battle to stay upright and to not fall is hard, and some days nearly impossible. But I thank you Heavenly Father for your word that says: "I can do all things through Christ that strengthens me." Lord, I need your help to daily keep from falling. So Lord, I honor and acknowledge you now and your ability to help me. And I receive your help today and each and every day of my life. For I cannot do it on my own. Thank you Lord, for your grace and mercy daily. In Jesus name I pray, Amen.

Day 17

Awaken Your Dreams

Ephesians 3:20 (KJV)
"Now unto him that is able to do exceeding abundantly above all that we ask or think, according to the power that worketh in us."

We as men all have dreams of what we want to do, like owning a business, becoming a teacher; a musician, an astronaut or a lawyer. We know that we need a plan to get there. But often life throws us for a loop, and we settle putting our dreams and things we want on the shelf. Have we as men ever thought that God has a plan for how we can get there? God wants us to live an abundant life, to accomplish our dreams and the things we want to do. But we as men must believe that he can do it. All it takes is allowing God to help you with it and standing on his word and promise. We must have the faith to know that with God we can do all things. So: write the vision, awaken your dreams, set up a plan to get there and watch God do it for you. The earth is the Lord's and the fullness thereof. If God said it, He will do it. Why should we as men disqualify ourselves when God says we qualify? For all things are possible to them that believe. So, don't just have faith the size of a mustard seed, but also have the faith to tell the mountain be thou removed and be cast into the sea. With that kind of faith, everything we want to do and dream of doing can come to pass. We as men must step up to the challenge of awakening our dreams and allow God to give us the wisdom to get there. For if we do the little things, God is able to do the big things in our dreams and lives, the start of it is: First we must believe. Believe that God can do it and believe that our dreams can come to pass. And know that it's never too late to make our dreams a reality.

Prayer of the Day

Father, you said in your word that you want me to prosper even as my soul. So Lord, I pray that every dream and vision you have given come to pass. Give me the wisdom, the plan, the where and how I get started. Connect me with people who will propel me to my dream, vision and destiny. I stand on your word and promise, and I know you will take care of me. In Jesus name I pray, Amen.

Day 18

Son, Don't Give Up On Me

Isaiah 40:31 (ESV)
"But they who wait for the LORD shall renew their strength; they shall mount up with wings like eagles; they shall run and not be weary; they shall walk and not faint."

God's message to you Man of Valor today is: 'Son, Don't Give Up On Me.' There have been many times that you have been hurt and many times that you have been deceived. There have been times that you have been greatly disappointed by those in whom you have placed your trust and hope. You may have followed many who abused you, tried to control you, manipulate you and take advantage of you. But the Lord was still there with you. He cried when you cried. He was angry when things were done unto you. He did not just sit back and watch all that happened. He was behind the scenes dealing on your behalf. There were times when you couldn't take it anymore. There were times you fled away and closed off your heart, soul and spirit. There may have been times that you turned your back on God himself. There were times of confusion, when you were wounded, torn and not trusting again. Many times you lost yourself in the process and even lost relationships. Most importantly your relationship with

God sometimes suffered. In response to this, God wants to encourage you 'Today' not to give up on him. He wants you to know that he never intended for you to go through many of the things you went through. He never has turned his back on you. He wants you to understand that he was never in the abuse, the hurt, the wounds, the lies nor the deception. He saw what happened to you and in many situations and circumstances he did protect you. He shall avenge you. He shall take care of those things that concern you. He is continuously behind the scenes working and moving on your behalf. Even in the times that you feel alone and times where it seems like God is so quiet. He never leaves you. He never forsakes you, and he never gives up on you. And he doesn't want you to give up on him. He is sending encouragement your way 'Today' not to give up on him. You are connected to a God who is love, truth, comfort, healing, deliverance, freedom and peace. He is your strong tower, your avenger, your protector, your Savior and Lord. And he encourages you today to turn back unto him. You will not regret your decision.

Prayer of the Day

Lord, I am hurting, and I am in need of healing. Lord, I don't know where to turn. You are my only hope. Lord, please forgive me for giving up on you. Lord, please forgive me for not seeking your help. Lord, please restore and heal me and help me not to walk away from you again. Help me to seek after you no matter what happens. Help me to know that you are there always no matter where I am. I love you Lord. In Jesus name I pray, Amen.

_____
_____
_____
_____
_____
_____
_____
_____
_____
_____
_____
_____
_____
_____
_____
_____
_____
_____
_____
_____
_____
_____
_____

Day 19

A New Day, A New Man

2 Corinthians 5:17 (KJV)
"Therefore, if any man be in Christ, he is a new creature: old things passed away; behold all things are become new."

For so long in our lives we have felt like we can't be the Men that God wants us to be. Live life to the fullest. Being constantly reminded of our past failures, past hurts, what we lack and past shame. But the time is now for us to move forward. For this important scripture is a way that Christ is telling us that he paid the price with his blood and to know that we as men are Free! Free from the past and no longer have to hold on to it. We don't have to be reminded of our past hurts, failures and sin for it is in Christ that we have been transformed and become a new creature. We should no longer revert back to our old selves who hold on to bitterness, resentment, depression. Feeling like we as men can't amount to anything. At times, we feel like we don't matter. We have had some people in our lives tell us that we would be this same person throughout our years and never move forward. God is saying in Ephesians 4:22-24; that we put off the former conversation: the old man, which is corrupt according to the deceitful lust. And be renewed in the spirit of your mind. That we put on the new man, which after God is created in righteousness and true holiness. It's time for us as men to let go of everything that has had us bound and be free. Transformed and renewed in our hearts, minds and spirits. And be the man that God created us to be. Don't hold on to our old and former selves any longer. Embrace a new life in Christ Jesus. We as men must forgive ourselves and give ourselves a fresh start. So, let this day be a new day and we become a new man.

Prayer of the Day

Lord, I thank you for paying the price with your blood and showing me that I no longer have to hold on to my past; letting it dictate my future. You have shown me that there's new life in you, and I can be transformed by your word. I can be the man that you want me to be. Lord everything that I allowed to keep me from moving forward in you I let it go right now. Take off the former things of me and embrace the new me that lives a life pleasing to you. In Jesus name I pray, Amen.

Day 20

Your High Position Before God

James 1:9 (NIV)
"The brother in humble circumstances ought to take pride in his high position"

With God, your obedience, your sacrifice, your labor, your travail and your dying to flesh is your high position in the eyes of God. God esteems those of us in these places higher than those who operate in pride. Your lowly state is your high place. It's your greatest place. At this level no man can take away God's favor from you. His hand from over your life, and his blessings that He has in store for you. Nor can they take away His call upon your life His purpose and provision for you. You are indeed blessed; you cannot be cursed. Where you may had been once last, you are now first. Where you may have been once the tail, you are now the head. Where you may have once seemed to trail through hell, you are already being elevated in the spirit. When it may have once seemed like you were dead, you are already alive. From this place, others will benefit from your experience and will learn of Christ through you. Man of Valor, you are moving from your pain to God's promises. You are moving from being weak to becoming strong; from experiencing failures to experiencing successes. Man of Valor, you are greater than he that subdues in pride. In the story of

Joseph, Joseph in the beginning was sold as a slave. They bruised his feet with shackles and his neck was put in irons; Till what he foretold came to pass and till the word of the Lord proved him true" (Psalms 105:16-19). Joseph was being led into a high position. It was there that he was prepared to be the most powerful man in the world as a thirty-year old. He learned many things about God during captivity that were used later as he ruled over a nation. God's encouragement to you today is for you Man of Valor, to find yourself in humble circumstances taking pride in your high position. For the Lord says: "You are greater than he that subdues in pride. You are greater than the arrogant one. You are greater than the fool. Great is your position in my kingdom because of Me. Son, I am pleased to call you mine, says the Lord."

Prayer of the Day

Heavenly Father, thank you for helping me to truly understand what being in a high position means. Forgive me for any times when I exalted myself in pride before man. Lord, thank you for helping me to become humble and understanding what true humility is. Lord, I am proud to be called your son and I am proud to call you my Father. Lord, help me daily to remain humble and to see all my humbling circumstances and situations as high positions before you. In Jesus name I pray, Amen.

Day 21

NO Cross, NO Crown

Romans 8:17 (KJV)
"And if children, then heirs; heirs of God, and joint-
heirs with Christ; if so be that we suffer with him, that
we may be also glorified together. "

We as Men must walk in our power and authority in
Christ. For we are the children of God; therefore we
are heirs and joint- heirs of God. But we never
realize and recognize the power that is within us. We
as men need to be more in the things of God to know
more of who He is so that we know who we are. Our
problem is the time in which we live. We as men
want everything so easy with no struggle. We want
all the success, but not the knowledge it takes to
achieve and be a good steward of it.
You cannot go for the crown, if you don't go through
the process of getting it. Just like a teacher can't be
a teacher without going through schooling and
graduating. In order to teach others, so that the ones
we teach can be educated and secure their future.
We as men always look at most successful people
on TV and the media and want to be like them.
Wondering how did they make it? But we never sit
down with them to hear the story of how they went
from ordinary to great success. There's an old

saying, "You see me in my glory but you don't know my story." In order for us as men to be great in everything we ask or want to be, we must go through the process. It may not always be easy but just know that with God we can make it even though. We are being tried through the fire but we're coming out of it as pure gold. And that is a win-win.

Prayer of the Day

Lord, in everything that I want to do or be help me through the process. Be my strength in times that I am weak and want to quit. Help me and to know that you are with me. Let everything that I do give you the glory, honor and the praise. In Jesus name I pray, Amen.

Day 22

Plan and Prepare Ahead

Proverbs 6:6-8 (NIV)
"Go to the ant, you sluggard; consider its ways and be wise! It has no commander, no overseer or ruler, yet it stores its provisions in summer and gathers its food at harvest."

Man of Valor, you are like the ant, and the Word of God encourages you to be like the ant. Consider the ant's ways. Ants are small and tiny; sometimes you can barely see them. Though small, they are smart and wise in their ways. One ant usually goes in search for food, and upon finding it, it goes back to its habitat and gets others to come to the harvest. Sometimes it partakes of the food where it finds it, but other times the other ants help carry the food back to its habitat and they partake of it there. The most important thing to understand about an ant, is that it uses the summer months to begin storing up food. It realizes that winter is coming and it must store up in order to survive during the winter months. Ants, spend their time making the smart choices when it matters in order to enjoy the harvest in due season. In this season, Man of Valor, it is important that you consider your decisions. It's important to make sure that provision is made in order to produce a harvest. God, when he formed and made you, gave you no commander, no overseer, and no ruler.

He placed much power in your hand to get wealth. He tells you in the book of Proverbs, that if you seek God for wisdom, that you shall find it and have it. That if you bind it to your heart, that you shall never be without it. Within God's wisdom is the answer of how to obtain provision for the harvest that you shall store up. Also that you are able to gather and partake of your harvest in due season. So Man of Valor, will you do what is wise in this season as your progress forward through the seasons. Will you be wise as the ant? –Selah

Prayer of the Day

Lord, you are my God that loves me and wishes me to prosper in all that I do. Please forgive me for any times that I have been like a sluggard. Lord, thank you for reminding me that I need to be like the ant and be wise in all my ways. Father, you have given me great wisdom through your word. Now, I ask that you would help me to store up provisions while it is summer in order that I may reap food at harvest time. Help me not to do anything to prolong the harvest any longer. But teach me in order that I may know what I must do to prepare. In Jesus name I pray, Amen.

Day 23

Men of Humility

1 Peter 5:6 (KJV)
"Humble yourselves therefore under the mighty hand of God, that he may exalt you in due time."

The word God says, that we as men should humble ourselves under the mighty hand of God and he will exalt us in due time, But the problem is that we as men don't stay humble enough so that we can be exalted. Especially living in this microwave world we always gotta have it as soon as possible and then get frustrated when we don't get it. Everyone wants the exaltation, but they're not willing to go through the process. We as men all want to be recognized, promoted, praised and honored. It is God who has given us that blessing. We end up forgetting what God did for us and we go around as though we made it possible by ourselves. We act like we are all that and a bag of chips. Then we lose the purpose and reason why he gave us that blessing in the first place. God gave the blessing so he can get the glory out of it and us. We as men need to put our pride and arrogance aside and stop doing what the enemy wants us to do. We become prideful and arrogant and think we did it. We admire ourselves like Satan did and got cast out of heaven. We as men need to continue to be the vessel that God can use and not be the one that is selfish. Because without God we

55

are nothing and can do nothing. We as men need to remember that he is the author and finisher of our faith.

Prayer of the Day

Father, help me to stay humble and have a grateful heart. Help me to continue to stay humble at home, on my job and any place that I may go. Help me to show humility to others, so I can be the vessel that you can use. May everything that I do give you all the glory. For without you I am nothing. In Jesus name I pray, Amen

Day 24

Avoid Bad Company

Proverbs 4:10 (NIV)
"Listen, my son, accept what I say, and the years of
your life will be many."

Man of Valor, "Do not set foot on the path of the
wicked or walk in the way of evil men. Avoid it, do
not travel on it; turn from it and go on your way." -
Proverbs 4:14-15. We live in a generation where we
all want someone to call a friend. We all want that
person we can share our life experiences with,
someone to encourage us, be there for us, someone
that will have our back, someone to hang out with
and etc. God made us with that desire for friendship.
God made relationships because he understood that
we would need them. He even tells us in the word to
be accountable to one another and to share our
faults with one another in order that we may be
healed- James 5:16. So God designed us to have
relationships. Even as we desire friendships and
relationships, we must indeed be careful whom we
choose. There are many evil wicked people in earth
that seek to do us harm; they mean us no good. We
must make decisions not to walk in the ways of nor
associate ourselves with those that associate with
evil or live evil ways. Man of Valor, you are called to
a higher standard of living. You are worth more than
evil. Man of Valor, you are better than that. Good

always wins over evil and good portrays the very character of Christ. So Man of Valor, will you make the choice to listen and accept God's instructions in order that the years of your life may be longer? Will you decide to make the right choices for your life? Will you rid yourself if you have not already of the evil men or connections in your life? Make your decision today!

Prayer of the Day

Lord, help me to examine my friends and connections in this hour. Lord, I choose not to walk in the ways of the wicked nor connect myself with those who practice evil ways. Lord, help me to rid myself and cut off those connections, as I seek to live for you. Lord, help me daily to live up to the standard in which you are calling for me to live. Help me in all my decision making and Lord please place the right people in my life that should be in this season. Thank you Lord for being my best friend. I love you. In Jesus name I pray, Amen

Day 25

Men, Don't Lose Your Cool

Proverbs 15:1 (KJV)
"A soft answer turneth away wrath: but grievous words stir up anger."

Men, this is one emotion we are all most familiar with. When we get angry and lose our cool, we definitely don't think straight. This causes us to be in a big mess that we can't clean up. It's important that we as men must learn to be men that are slow to anger and resist strife. And not be the men who stir up strife. Just as God is gracious, full of compassion, slow to anger and of great mercy for us, we as men need to be the same for others. We must understand that God uses the weak things to show the strong and the foolish things to confound the wise. It is said in his word in Proverbs 22:8, "He that sows iniquity shall reap vanity: and the rod of his anger shall fail." And in Proverbs 22:11 says "He that loveth pureness of heart, for the grace of his lips the King shall be his friend." So we as men need to be the type of men to keep the peace and not create a war. Whether it is in our homes, on our jobs or with other people. We need to be the men who don't crack under pressure and get angry but be the men who are cool and smooth as ice.

Prayer of the Day

Father, help me to be the man that is gracious,
shows compassion and gives grace to others.
Whether I am at home, at work or anywhere that I
go. Help me to be the one who has a pure heart and
be a man of peace. Not a man of war. Help me to be
the one who can make a difference in the lives of
others. In Jesus name I pray, Amen.

Day 26

Check Your Armor

Ephesians 6:10-18 (KJV)
"Be strong in the Lord and in the power of His might.
Put on the whole armor of God that you may be able
to stand against the wiles of the devil. For we do not
wrestle against flesh and blood, but against
principalities, against powers, against the rulers of
the darkness of this age, against spiritual hosts of
wickedness in the heavenly places. Take up the
whole armor of God that you may be able to
withstand in the evil day, and having done all, to
stand. Stand therefore, having girded your waist with
truth, having put on the breastplate of righteousness,
and having shod your feet with the preparation of the
gospel of peace; above all, taking the shield of faith
with which you will be able to quench all the fiery
darts of the wicked one. "And take the helmet of
salvation, and the sword of the Spirit, which is the
word of God; praying always with all prayer and
supplication in the Spirit, being watchful to this end
with all perseverance and supplication for all the
saints."

Man of Valor, each and every day you wake up.
Along with putting on your physical clothes and
taking care of your physical body, you must also put
on your spiritual armor. Each and every day we step

outside our home, we may have our physical selves together. But what about spiritually and mentally? The Word of God is our daily bread and it is important that we read it every day. It is important that we put on our spiritual armor which protects us spiritually. For the enemy prowls around like a roaring lion, seeking whom he may devour. It's when you least expect it, that you tend to get caught spiritually off guard. That's what we need the greatest protection of. Mentally, you need to be engaged in what's in front of you and what's ahead of you that sometimes you can't even see. You need to be in tune with the Holy Spirit who is able to make you aware of all things. So be sure Man of Valor, that along with your physical preparations daily that you also prepare spiritually. By putting on the full armor of God that you may be prepared for things to come your way. –Selah

Prayer of the Day

Heavenly Father in the name of Jesus, I pray daily that the Word of God would serve as my reminder to put on my spiritual armor as I put on my natural clothes. Daily as I gear up and prepare for my day, help me to acknowledge you in prayer and to spend a few minutes in your word. Help me to allow every area of my spiritual being to be covered under your blood of protection. Help me to daily be aware of the attacks of the enemy and not take for granted Your presence. Thank you Lord for daily covering and protecting me. In Jesus name I pray, Amen.

_____
_____
_____
_____
_____
_____
_____
_____
_____
_____
_____
_____
_____
_____
_____
_____
_____
_____
_____
_____

Day 27

You Can't Tell Everyone Your Dreams

Genesis 37:5 (KJV)
"And Joseph dreamed a dream, and he told his brethren and they hated him yet the more."

We as men must understand that we can't tell our dreams to everyone. Even though there will be some who will be happy, excited and proud of us, There are some who will be jealous and start to dislike us. Some people will try to discourage us and sabotage us from allowing our dreams to come to pass. Yes. And also steal our dreams and ideas that God gave to us. It's important that we as men be careful of who we tell our dreams to. Because not everyone will be able to handle it. We must use discernment and allow the Holy Spirit to let us know who we can tell them to, and who we can connect with. We as men need to surround ourselves with people who will help make our dreams a reality. People who will build us up and not tear us down. People who will encourage us to make our dreams come true. So we as men must not allow the ones who are jealous and don't want to be happy for us to get in the way of our dreams. We must continue to move forward to the dreams, vision and ideas that God has given us.

Prayer of the Day

Lord, help me to be careful to whom I tell my ideas, visions and dreams to. Surround me with people who will be happy and support me and not discourage and tear me down. Surround me with people who will: build me up, encourage me and help me not to quit. But keep me working towards the dreams that you have for me. In Jesus name I pray, Amen.

Day 28

Close The Doors

Philippians 3:13 (KJV)
"No, dear brothers and sisters, I have not achieved
it, but I focus on this one thing: Forgetting the past
and looking forward to what lies ahead,"

I the Lord, am calling forth the closing of many doors
in the lives of my people. I am sending forth my word
to you Man of Valor to help you see the door(s)
which I desire to be closed. The enemy has been
allowed to come in and to destroy the desires, hearts
and souls of my people. Through sins, temptations
and through false imitations of me. My voice among
them has been diminished greatly, and they no
longer hear me. But they hear the voices of others.
Many of my people have resorted back to the past to
try and heal and redeem themselves. They have
gone back and pried open doors that I have once
closed. They have resurrected people whom I have
once cut out of their lives. They have opened the
door for them to re-enter their lives knowing what the
result will be. Why? Because they have given up on
me. They have gone blind and they have lost their
faith. Right now is not a time for being comfortable
but it is a time to press. One must press in order to
continue on strong until the end of their faith. They
will come against many battles and circumstances
that they must fight. Therefore, there is no time to get

comfortable. Only I the Lord can give them peace and comfort within themselves. Knowing that I am ultimately in control over all and that they are not alone and can fight. There is nothing too hard for me to do. Even the more, they can arise with strength and walk in boldness. Knowing that there is nothing that they can't do in my name. I, their God will give them strength and instruction on how to live. So the unsaved boyfriends, the on the side lovers, the family member(s) that seem to be controlling your life, They All Must Go Now. You cannot let them to continue to stay. You cannot let them rule and abide in your life. You must close the door once again. You must allow me to be God and deal with them. You must allow me the Lord your God to provide for what you need. Where I have told you 'No' to certain things, you must trust me in my answer. Continue to trust that I have something better for you. You must understand that even what I am asking you to do right now is for your good. It is healthy and it is part of my great plan and will for your life. I am removing all unhealthy connections out of your life in order that you may be healthy. Man of Valor, you can choose this day to return unto me and allow me to shut those doors in your life. There is a great mandate on your life that I have sent, I will be with you and help you fulfill it. I need now for you to agree. Will you agree?

Prayer of the Day

Lord Heavenly Father, it is so hard to close doors sometimes of people in your life. It's so hard to cut off some connections. So Lord, I recognize that I need your help. Please help me to do what I know I need to do but can't seem to do myself. I allow you full control of my life because I acknowledge you as Lord. Thank you for closing these doors to restore only positive connections in my life. In Jesus name I pray, Amen.

_____
_____
_____
_____
_____
_____
_____
_____
_____
_____
_____
_____
_____
_____
_____
_____
_____
_____
_____
_____
_____
_____

Day 29

God's Servitude

Matthew 23:11 (KJV)
But he that is the greatest among you shall be your servant.
One of my favorite scriptures is Matt 5:8 "Blessed are the pure at heart for they shall see God." We as Men must understand: that being the greatest is not having to be the strongest, the smartest, the most athletic or a superhero. It simply means: having a caring heart for God, having a desire to care for people. Having a heart to serve, feeding the hungry, taking care of the sick. Helping and encouraging the ones who are lonely, broken hearted, rejected, and the ones who need some guidance. We as men, who love God, will always want to hear God saying 'well done thou good and faithful servant.' But in order for God to be pleased with our lives we must learn to serve as Christ has served. To love and care for the ones who are in need. When we serve others, we also are serving Christ, (see Matt 25:40). It doesn't take a whole lot of money, but just a willing and obedient heart. To do what God tells us to do. Being God's hands and feet means we are servants of God and servants to others. That's what Christ means about being the greatest. We as men must serve not only our homes, but our schools, our churches, our jobs, our communities and our cities. Let's be men of servitude and live a life pleasing to God.

Prayer of the Day

Lord, help me to be a man who serves and who has the heart to love and care for others. Help me to be the one who serves in my home, my community and my city. I know that when I serve the ones that are in need that I also serve you. In Jesus name I pray, Amen.

Day 30

God's Love Makes The Difference

Matthew 22:37-40 (KJV)
"Jesus said unto him, thou shalt love the Lord thy God with all thy heart, all thy soul, and all thy mind, this is the first and great commandment and the second is like unto it, thou shalt love thy neighbor as thyself. On these two commandments hang all the law and the prophets."

In times we live in, 'love' has been a word that has been thrown around. We as men use the word for other things we love: our cars, suits, houses and other materialistic things. But when it comes to loving people, we're not good at showing it. Two things that Jesus said which summarizes the 'Ten Commandments.' One is to love God with all of our hearts, souls and our minds. Two, is to love others as we love ourselves. The first one to us is seen like there's no problem in that. Why not love the God who created us and the earth. The God who came down from divinity to humanity walked among us and taught us how to live. Out of love for us, he freely gave his life for us. To destroy the very thing that separated us, so that we can commune with him. But when it comes to loving each other the same way that Christ loves us, we fail at that. How is it that we can say 'We Love God,' but can't say two words to each other? We're so quick to dislike, despise and judge. We think we can read people so quick. We put them in a category without taking the time to get to know who they are and what they have been through. We can't even say a kind word to each other. Making judgments on appearance, knowledge or success. It is amazing how we say 'we're the hands and feet of God,' but we do more hurt and harm instead of lending a helping hand. It's amazing how us as men how we say 'We are men of God,' the light of the world. Yet instead of being a light to a darkened world in these dark times, we want to stay among other lights. Lights are meant to illuminate places that are dark. Which means they are spread out. We do a lot of talking, but not enough doing. Always concentrating on looking good, but not being good. God wants us to start being good and stop looking good. For we as men should not only be hearers of the word but also doers too. So men, it is time for us to step up to the challenge. Show others the love of God and let his love make the difference.

Prayer of the Day

Father, let your love be in me that I may be a reflection of you. Let that when others see me, that they see you, Jesus. Help me to be the man that loves others and loves my enemies. Allow your love to make such a difference that it changes the lives of others. In Jesus name I pray, Amen.

About the Authors

Erica Rutherford is an author, minister, musician, songwriter, praise dancer, praise and worship leader, speaker, teacher residing in Central Indiana with her husband, Lewis C Rutherford Jr. Erica is a motivated driven leader that has been called to encourage and empower the people of God in this hour through her music, teachings, dance and writings. Erica and her husband are currently working on their 1st CD, 2 song collaborations and their next book 'No More Egypt.'

Erica has traveled some of the world as a classical violinist. Erica now does freelance music in the genres of gospel, inspirational and jazz. In her free time, Erica enjoys crafting, knitting, video and board games, hanging with friends, learning new things and traveling.

Erica can be reached her Facebook account name: EricaGodschildRutherford, website: www.kingdomwritersbooks.wordpress.com and email: kingdomwriters2017@gmail.com . You can visit Amazon.com, Barnes&Noble.com or contact her personally to purchase her books.

Lewis C Rutherford Jr. is an minister, singer, songwriter, musician and author residing in central Indiana with his wife Erica A Rutherford. Lewis is a high energy passionate leader that is called to encourage and empower the people of God in this hour through his music, teachings and his writings. Lewis and his wife are currently working on their 1st CD, 2 song collaborations and their next book 'No More Egypt.'

Lewis has traveled the world participating in various music conferences and events. Lewis does freelance music mainly in the genres of inspirational, gospel and jazz. In his free time, Lewis enjoys video and board games, learning and trying new things, hanging with friends, and traveling.

Lewis can be reach at his Gmail account name: Gospodj@gmail.com or kingdomwriters2017@gmail.com , and website: www.kingdomwritersbooks.wordpress.com , you can visit Amazon.com, Barnes&Noble.com or contact him personally to purchase his books.